Poets

A BOOK OF POSTCARDS
Photographs by Jill Krementz

Pomegranate
SAN FRANCISCO

Pomegranate
Box 6099
Rohnert Park, CA 94927

Pomegranate Europe Ltd.
Fullbridge House, Fullbridge
Maldon, Essex CM9 7LE
England

ISBN 0-7649-0357-8
Pomegranate Catalog No. A888

© 1997 Jill Krementz
Text by Alan Bisbort

Pomegranate publishes books of
postcards on a wide range of subjects.
Please write to the publisher for more information.

Designed by Elizabeth Key
Printed in Korea
06 05 04 03 02 01 00 99 98 97   10 9 8 7 6 5 4 3 2 1

As a young woman, Jill Krementz quickly established herself as one of America's most talented photojournalists, displaying a passionate and unique visual style. Throughout the 1960s she worked as a reporter, columnist, and photographer for various New York–based publications—including the *New York Herald Tribune*, which hired her in 1964 as its first female (and youngest) staff photographer. It was in the 1960s that she also began photographing writers. From 1967 to 1968 she was the official photographer for the 92nd Street Poetry Center, and it was during this tenure that she took the photographs of Marianne Moore, W. H. Auden, Robert Lowell, Adrienne Rich, Anne Sexton, and W. S. Merwin that appear in this book of postcards. She met her husband, Kurt Vonnegut, in 1970 when she photographed him shortly after the publication of *Slaughterhouse-Five.* They live in New York City with their daughter, Lily.

For the past three and a half decades, Krementz has moved back and forth between two worlds. On the one hand, there are her best-selling photo-essay books for young people, including the "Very Young" and "How It Feels" series, which have inspired and informed generations of children. On the other hand, there are her photographs of writers, which have grown into a massive—and unrivaled—photographic archive of contemporary literary figures comprising sessions with more than 1,500 writers. Her collection is not just a visual feast for modern book lovers; it will surely serve as an invaluable resource for future scholars, not unlike Carl Van Vechten's photographic collection of Harlem Renaissance writers of the 1920s and 1930s.

Uncompromising and thorough in her preparation, Jill Krementz brings to each session a familiarity with her subject's work. "I don't consider myself a photographer," she says. "I'm a photojournalist, since I generally photograph people in their environments. I try to see beyond the moment and into the subject. I want to show the private side of people without violating their privacy, and without being too intrusive." This sensitivity allows her to enter the individual writer's world unobtrusively, often capturing what John Updike, in his introduction to her most recent book, *The Writer's Desk* (Random House, 1996), calls "an ordering and a purging and a bringing into the light that which had been hidden an hour before." Her photographs, writes Updike, "in all their variety of milieu and demeanor, generally show people at peace in their settings, their activity, and their poses."

Aside from the fact that many of the poets captured here are poet laureates, Nobel Prize winners, and/or camera-shy visionaries, their own "ordering and purging" of words is likely to take place anywhere and at any time. As Stanley Kunitz noted in an interview with the *Washington Post* when he was serving as Consultant in Poetry (now U.S. Poet Laureate), "Poets are not easily domesticated, they are sometimes impolite, and they can be outrageous; but they are also idealists and visionaries whose presence is needed through history to clear the air of corruption and hypocrisy, to mock oppressors, and to challenge spiritual apathy." These thirty unique portraits convey, with dignity and precision, this most necessary, if undomesticated, literary breed. ■

Poets

PHOTOGRAPHS BY JILL KREMENTZ

YUSEF KOMUNYAKAA, Provincetown, Mass., August 6, 1996

Yusef Komunyakaa (b. 1947) is the son of a Louisiana carpenter as well as a decorated Vietnam veteran. He chronicles the raw elements of his life with the controlled improvisation of a master jazzman. The titles of his collections—*Lost in the Bonewheel Factory* (1979), *Copacetic* (1984), *I Apologize for the Eyes in My Head* (1986), and *Neon Vernacular: New and Selected Poems* (1993)—evoke the spirit within.

POMEGRANATE BOX 6099 ROHNERT PARK CA 94927

© Jill Krementz

Poets

PHOTOGRAPHS BY JILL KREMENTZ

ADRIENNE RICH, New York, N.Y., April 22, 1968
Adrienne Rich (b. 1929) has undergone one of the most remarkable transformations in contemporary American poetry, moving from her "decorous" early verse to become what Sharon Olds calls "our Atlas, holding up not the heavens but the earth" and what the *New York Times* has called "the doyenne of a newly defined female literature." A public and private poet, Rich is also an activist, a teacher, and a translator. Her works include *Diving into the Wreck* (1973), *Of Woman Born* (1976), *The Dream of a Common Language* (1978), and *An Atlas of the Difficult World* (1991).

POMEGRANATE BOX 6099 ROHNERT PARK CA 94927

© Jill Krementz

Poets

PHOTOGRAPHS BY JILL KREMENTZ

MARK DOTY (with his golden retriever Beau),
Provincetown, Mass., August 6, 1996
Mark Doty (b. 1953) is in love with "the language of the day's ten thousand aspects," and his four books of lush, graceful verse have put him in the top rank of American poets. Each of Doty's poems is a verbal still life, a life-affirming flower amidst the forest of the AIDS plague that is never far from his field of vision. His books *My Alexandria* (1993) and *Atlantis* (1995) carried on in the wake of tragedy, creating what one poem calls a "vast conjugation of the verb *to shine.*"

POMEGRANATE BOX 6099 ROHNERT PARK CA 94927

© Jill Krementz

Poets

PHOTOGRAPHS BY JILL KREMENTZ

ANNE SEXTON and W. S. MERWIN, New York, N.Y., November 11, 1968
Anne Sexton (1928–1974) and W. S. Merwin (b. 1927) are poets of intel-
lectual depth and formal sophistication whose verse pushes the boundaries
of language. Sexton struggled with "madness" most of her adult life, a
literary battle that began with *To Bedlam and Part Way Back* (1960) and
ended with the posthumous *The Awful Rowing Toward God* (1975).
Merwin, a prolific poet and translator, now lives in Hawaii, where he has
created a remarkable nature preserve and forest. His *Selected Poems* was
published in 1988.

POMEGRANATE BOX 6099 ROHNERT PARK CA 94927

© Jill Krementz

Poets

PHOTOGRAPHS BY JILL KREMENTZ

ROBERT PINSKY, Saratoga Springs, N.Y., July 8, 1996
Robert Pinsky (b. 1940) has said, "I am interested in the truth of things
not symbolically but actually," and this quest has ranged through five
volumes of poetry and three books of essays on poetry and down into his
verse translation of *The Inferno of Dante* (1994). *The Figured Wheel: New
and Collected Poems, 1966–1996* (1996) is a generous anthology of his
first four books, including *An Explanation of America* (1980) and *History
of My Heart* (1984).

POMEGRANATE BOX 6099 ROHNERT PARK CA 94927

© Jill Krementz

Poets

PHOTOGRAPHS BY JILL KREMENTZ

LOUISE GLÜCK, Saratoga Springs, N.Y., July 8, 1996
Louise Glück (b. 1943) is a poet of stunning precision and honesty
whose six books of highly acclaimed verse and collection *The Wild Iris*
(1992) testify to her observation that "deceit begins as forgetting."
A serious teacher and student of poetry, Glück has also published to
critical acclaim a book of essays on the craft, *Proofs and Theories* (1994).
She credits Stanley Kunitz with reminding her of the "lost perception"
that "whatever the truth is, to speak it is a great adventure."

POMEGRANATE BOX 6099 ROHNERT PARK CA 94927

© Jill Krementz

Poets

PHOTOGRAPHS BY JILL KREMENTZ

JAMES MERRILL, Stonington, Conn., June 14, 1973

James Merrill (1926–1995) was a master poet of elegant verse. While he also wrote two novels, three plays, and two books of prose—including a touching memoir, *A Different Person* (1993)—Merrill was preeminently a poet. Among his verse collections are *Nights and Days* (1966), *Braving the Elements* (1972), *Divine Comedies* (1976), and *Mirabell: Books of Numbers* (1978). In an early poem, "Foliage of Vision," he announced his vision: "The act by which we see / Is both the landscape-gardening of our dreams / And the root's long revel under the clipped lawn."

POMEGRANATE BOX 6099 ROHNERT PARK CA 94927

© Jill Krementz

Poets

PHOTOGRAPHS BY JILL KREMENTZ

ANTHONY HECHT, Washington, D.C., May 4, 1995
Anthony Hecht (b. 1923) is a poet of astonishing dexterity whose verse challenges the mind while charging the imagination. His "imperial command" of image and form were evident in his first book, *A Summoning of Stones* (1954), and are in full bloom in *The Hard Hours* (1967) and *The Venetian Vespers* (1980). Hecht was Consultant in Poetry (now Poet Laureate) at the Library of Congress in 1982–1984.

POMEGRANATE BOX 6099 ROHNERT PARK CA 94927

© Jill Krementz

Poets

PHOTOGRAPHS BY JILL KREMENTZ

RITA DOVE, Charlottesville, Va., March 4, 1995
Rita Dove (b. 1952) was appointed U.S. Poet Laureate in 1993, and she took
to the job with a contagious joy seldom seen in government service. Her
books include a poetry collection, *The Yellow House on the Corner* (1980);
a volume of short stories, *Fifth Sunday* (1985); a novel, *Through the Ivory
Gate* (1992); a verse play, *The Darker Face of the Earth* (1994); and *Thomas
and Beulah* (1986), the verse story of her grandparents. She is seen here in
her beloved cabin, where she writes.

POMEGRANATE BOX 6099 ROHNERT PARK, CA 94927

© Jill Krementz

Poets

PHOTOGRAPHS BY JILL KREMENTZ

PABLO NERUDA, Paris, France, February 3, 1972

Pablo Neruda (Neftalí Ricardo Reyes Basoalto) (1904–1973) created immense, prophetic, and romantic poetry that earned him the Nobel Prize in literature in 1971. The essential strength and humanity of his verse are evident in masterworks such as *Residencia en la tierra* (1925–1935) and *Canto general* (1943). A man of conscience as well as Chile's greatest man of letters, Neruda suffered for his activism and socialist views. In accepting his Nobel Prize, he said, "We must travel across lonely and rugged terrain, through isolation and silence, to reach the magic zone where we can dance an awkward dance or sing a melancholy song." He is seen here, as Chile's ambassador to France, with his favorite shell.

POMEGRANATE BOX 6099 ROHNERT PARK CA 94927

© Jill Krementz

Poets

PHOTOGRAPHS BY JILL KREMENTZ

ROBERT HASS, Washington, D.C., June 19, 1996
Robert Hass (b. 1941), critic and translator, has an unabashed love of the
written word that crosses literary genres and language barriers. He is best
known for his poetry—*Field Guide* (1973), *Praise* (1979), *Human Wishes*
(1989), and *Sun Under Wood* (1996)—for which he was selected by the
Librarian of Congress to be U.S. Poet Laureate in 1995–1997.

POMEGRANATE BOX 6099 ROHNERT PARK CA 94927

© Jill Krementz

Poets

PHOTOGRAPHS BY JILL KREMENTZ

MARK STRAND, JOSEPH BRODSKY, ADAM ZAGAJEWSKI, and
DEREK WALCOTT, New York, N.Y., January 18, 1986
Mark Strand (b. 1934), Joseph Brodsky (1940–1996), Adam Zagajewski
(b. 1945), and Derek Walcott (b. 1930) came to the United States from
all points of the compass: Canada, St. Lucia, Poland, and the Soviet
Union, respectively. Among them, they hold two Nobel Prizes (Walcott
and Brodsky), two U.S. Poet Laureateships (Strand and Brodsky), and
numerous other awards, honors, and chairs. They are gathered here in
the garden of Brodsky's Greenwich Village townhouse while attending
the International P.E.N. Conference.

POMEGRANATE · BOX 6099 · ROHNERT PARK, CA 94927

© Jill Krementz

Poets

PHOTOGRAPHS BY JILL KREMENTZ

JOHN ASHBERY, New York, N.Y., March 14, 1995
John Ashbery (b. 1927) has charmed, baffled, provoked, and moved
readers while immeasurably expanding the boundaries of modern poetry.
An eminent art critic as well as a novelist, playwright, translator, and
professor, he writes with the unpredictable, constantly shifting perceptions
of a painter. His best-known collection, *Self-Portrait in a Convex Mirror*
(1975), was inspired by the Renaissance painter Parmigianino. He is seen
here in his Chelsea apartment sitting beneath *The Painting Table,* a 1954
work by close friend Jane Freilicher.

POMEGRANATE BOX 6099 ROHNERT PARK CA 94927

© Jill Krementz

Poets

PHOTOGRAPHS BY JILL KREMENTZ

S H A R O N   O L D S, New York, N.Y., February 18, 1993

Sharon Olds (b. 1942) is a poet of uncommon power who transforms the fleeting moments of her life into shards of startling beauty, all the while leaving herself open to surprising and often painful epiphanies. Among her best-known works are *The Dead and the Living* (1984) and *The Father* (1992), a chronicle of her father's slow death from cancer that manages to be humbling, loving, and life-affirming.

POMEGRANATE   BOX 6099   ROHNERT PARK   CA   94927

© Jill Krementz

Poets

PHOTOGRAPHS BY JILL KREMENTZ

PHILIP LEVINE, New York, N.Y., September 26, 1995
Philip Levine (b. 1928) is a poet of deep social conscience whose early
experience as an industrial worker in Detroit instilled in him a passionate
commitment to the lives of America's workers who, he said, "weren't being
heard." In the tradition of Walt Whitman, he honors their daily toils, but
he also asks "Why?" In *What Work Is* (1991), he wrote, "Not the old why
of why must I spend five nights a week? Just, 'Why?'" Among his other
important books are *The Names of the Lost* (1976), a tribute to Spain's
anarchists of the 1930s, and *The Simple Truth* (1994).

POMEGRANATE BOX 6099 ROHNERT PARK CA 94927

© Jill Krementz

Poets

PHOTOGRAPHS BY JILL KREMENTZ

OCTAVIO PAZ, New York, N.Y., May 22, 1995
Octavio Paz (b. 1914), the greatest of Mexico's modernist literary figures, has written more than thirty books of poetry and thirty-five books of prose. He has called his life's work a quest "to produce a text which would be an intersection of poetry, narrative, and essay." It is precisely this uncategorizable quality—as much philosophy as poetics—that has made him a towering international figure. A bilingual edition of his *Collected Poems, 1957–1987* was published in 1987.

POMEGRANATE   BOX 6099   ROHNERT PARK CA 94927

© Jill Krementz

Poets

PHOTOGRAPHS BY JILL KREMENTZ

GARY SNYDER and ALLEN GINSBERG, New York, N.Y., May 18, 1988
Gary Snyder (b. 1930) and Allen Ginsberg (b. 1926) challenged the literary
establishment and captured the imagination of postwar America with their
raw and unrepentant Beat poetry. Never compromising their personal,
political, or spiritual ideals, they have doggedly pursued unique poetic
visions to become international literary figures and distinguished members
of the academy. Ginsberg's *Selected Poems* (1996) and Snyder's *Mountains
and Rivers Without End* (1996) are their most recent summary statements.

POMEGRANATE   BOX 6099   ROHNERT PARK CA 94927

© Jill Krementz

Poets

PHOTOGRAPHS BY JILL KREMENTZ

MARIANNE MOORE, New York, N.Y., November 17, 1967
Marianne Moore (1887–1972), editor, translator, Brooklyn Dodgers fan,
and above all a poet of force and intelligence, is seen here backstage at
the 92nd Street Poetry Center. Her *Collected Poems* (1951) remains a
monument for the age.

POMEGRANATE BOX 6099 ROHNERT PARK CA 94927

© Jill Krementz

Poets

PHOTOGRAPHS BY JILL KREMENTZ

CZESLAW MILOSZ, New York, N.Y., January 8, 1986
Czeslaw Milosz (b. 1911) is one of our century's greatest, and least embittered, poets of witness. Born in Lithuania, he survived five years of Nazi occupation in Warsaw only to be put "under the domination of Moscow"—a totalitarian epoch he chronicled in *The Captive Mind* (1953). He left Poland in 1951 and lived in Paris until 1960, when he took a professorship at the University of California, Berkeley, where he remained until his retirement. *The Collected Poems, 1931–1987* offers a representative sample of his work. In the poem "December 1," he writes, "I describe this for I have learned to doubt philosophy / And the visible world is all that remains." Milosz received the Nobel Prize in literature in 1980.

POMEGRANATE BOX 6099 ROHNERT PARK CA 94927

© Jill Krementz

Poets

PHOTOGRAPHS BY JILL KREMENTZ

STANLEY KUNITZ, Provincetown, Mass., August 6, 1996
Stanley Kunitz (b. 1905) is one of this century's true gentlemen of letters,
and a revered teacher and generous mentor to countless younger poets.
He was selected as Consultant in Poetry (now Poet Laureate) at the Library
of Congress in 1974–1976. He published his most recent book, *Passing
Through,* in 1995, at the age of ninety. A noted horticulturist, he's seen
here in his garden.

POMEGRANATE   BOX 6099   ROHNERT PARK CA 94927

© Jill Krementz

Poets

PHOTOGRAPHS BY JILL KREMENTZ

ROBERT LOWELL, New York, N.Y., April 22, 1968
Robert Lowell (1917–1977) devoted his life to poetry and became one of
America's most conscientious literary figures. A tireless teacher, translator,
reader, and writer of poetry, Lowell was widely honored for his efforts.
Among Lowell's greatest works are *Lord Weary's Castle* (1946) and *Life
Studies* (1959). He reflected on his inner struggles in the poem "Last
Things, Black Pines at 4 A.M.": "Even the best writer in his best lines / is
incurably imperfect, crying for truth, knowledge, / honesty, inspiration he
cannot have."

POMEGRANATE BOX 6099 ROHNERT PARK CA 94927

© Jill Krementz

Poets

PHOTOGRAPHS BY JILL KREMENTZ

CAROLYN FORCHÉ, Saratoga Springs, N.Y., July 8, 1996
Carolyn Forché (b. 1950) has been hailed by a chorus as diverse as Jacobo
Timerman, who compared her to Pablo Neruda, and Margaret Atwood,
who called hers "a poetry of courage and passion, which manages to be
tender and achingly sensual." Both her work and her life are driven by an
unflagging commitment to human rights. Her books include *Gathering the
Tribes* (1975) and *The Country Between Us* (1981), one of contemporary
poetry's best-selling collections.

POMEGRANATE BOX 6099 ROHNERT PARK CA 94927

© Jill Krementz

Poets

PHOTOGRAPHS BY JILL KREMENTZ

W. H. AUDEN, New York, N.Y., November 6, 1967

W. H. Auden (1907–1973) wrote that he would have preferred to write "in the old grand manner, / Out of a resonant heart," but, as his editor Edward Mendelson said, "He was the first poet writing in English who felt at home in the twentieth century. He welcomed into his poetry all the disordered conditions of his time." Auden was his generation's most influential poet. Because he went his own idiosyncratic way, his "rigorous honesty" continues to delight succeeding generations.

POMEGRANATE BOX 6099 ROHNERT PARK CA 94927

© Jill Krementz

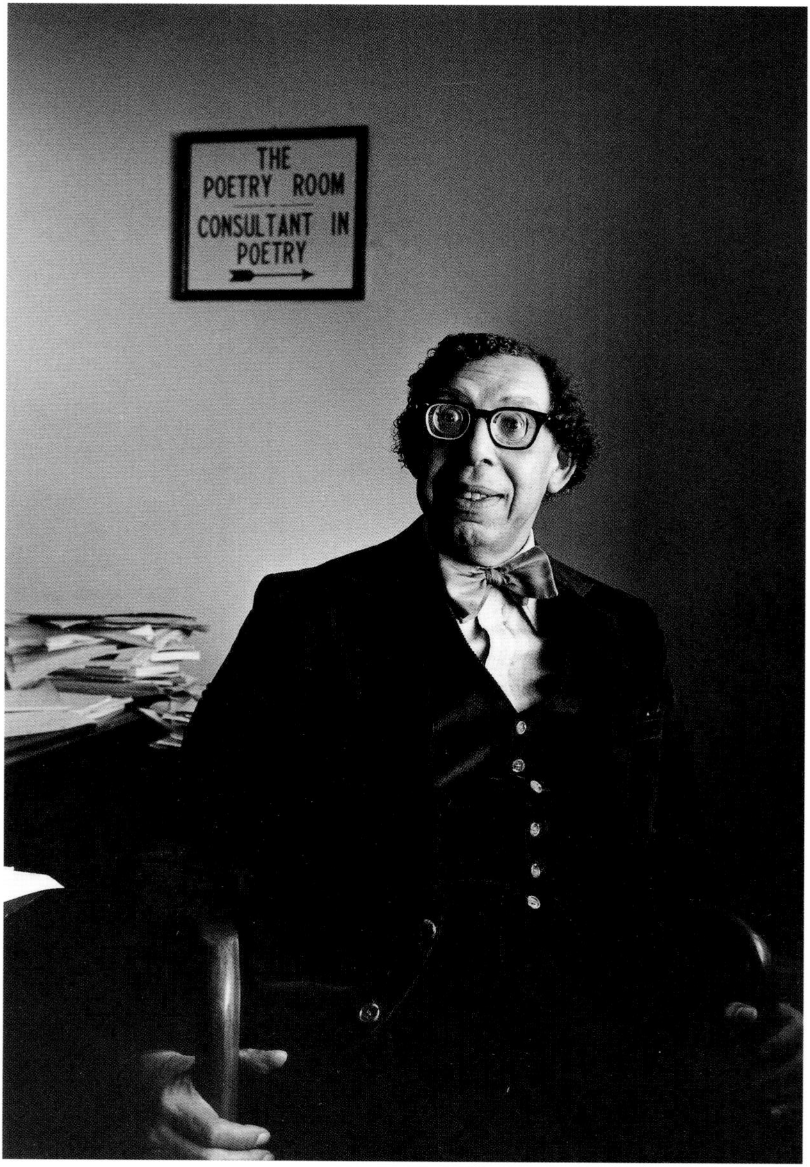
THE
POETRY ROOM
CONSULTANT IN
POETRY

Poets

PHOTOGRAPHS BY JILL KREMENTZ

ROBERT HAYDEN, Washington, D.C., October 27, 1976
Robert Hayden (1913–1980) was the first African American to be
named Consultant in Poetry (now Poet Laureate) at the Library of
Congress. His poetic voice, rooted in black experience, had a universal
vision that resounded with power in such works as *A Ballad of
Remembrance* (1962) and *Words in the Mourning Time* (1970).

POMEGRANATE BOX 6099 ROHNERT PARK CA 94927

© Jill Krementz

Poets

PHOTOGRAPHS BY JILL KREMENTZ

ROBERT BLY, New York, N.Y., April 11, 1996

Although Robert Bly (b. 1926) is known to millions as an elder of the men's movement and the best-selling author of *Iron John: A Book About Men* (1990), he has been one of America's most celebrated poets and translators for almost four decades. He came to public attention as editor of an influential journal, *The Sixties,* and author of *The Light Around the Body* (1967). Since his friend William Stafford's death in 1993, Bly has honored him by writing a poem every morning. "I write in bed," he says, "and don't get up until the poem is done."

Pomegranate Box 6099 Rohnert Park, CA 94927

© Jill Krementz

Poets

PHOTOGRAPHS BY JILL KREMENTZ

MURIEL RUKEYSER, New York, N.Y., April 18, 1974

Muriel Rukeyser (1913–1980) made her passions clear from the outset with *Theory of Flight* (1935), about which W. R. Benet said, "She is radical politically, but she writes as a poet, not a propagandist." Rukeyser spent the next half century joyfully assuming the role of "spokespoet," and her journeys of conscience were as large as her verse, which Richard Eberhart has called "primordial and torrential." Among her twenty collections are *Waterlily Fire: Poems 1935–1962* (1962) and *The Collected Poems* (1978).

POMEGRANATE BOX 6099 ROHNERT PARK CA 94927

© Jill Krementz

Poets

PHOTOGRAPHS BY JILL KREMENTZ

CHARLES SIMIC, New York, N.Y., May 15, 1996

Charles Simic (b. 1938) is a distinguished poet and professor who has used his own dark journey to "re-create the possibility of light upon the earth." His life is the stuff of epic poetry: childhood in war-torn Belgrade, adolescence in a totalitarian state, teen years as an immigrant to Paris and then to Chicago, and, finally, the rigors of adult assimilation into American culture. He not only made the transition heroically—writing in English and serving in the U.S. Army—but also brought notice to the work of Slavic poets as an award-winning translator. His books include *Charon's Cosmology* (1977) and *The World Doesn't End* (1989).

POMEGRANATE BOX 6099 ROHNERT PARK CA 94927

© Jill Krementz

Poets

PHOTOGRAPHS BY JILL KREMENTZ

RICHARD WILBUR, New York, N.Y., May 16, 1973

For half a century, Richard Wilbur (b. 1921) has stayed true to traditional rhyme and meter and eschewed "raw" first-person confessions for his own carefully "cooked" poetic vision. In the process, he has seen his star ascend both early and late in his career with his acclaimed books *Things of This World* (1957) and *New and Collected Poems* (1988). In between these high points, Wilbur deflected the fickleness of critics with his unanimously praised translations of Molière, Racine, and Voltaire. He was named U.S. Poet Laureate in 1987.

POMEGRANATE BOX 6099 ROHNERT PARK CA 94927

© Jill Krementz

Poets

PHOTOGRAPHS BY JILL KREMENTZ

LUCILLE CLIFTON, Columbia, Md., June 19, 1996
Lucille Clifton (b. 1936) has illuminated contemporary poetry with a
"fierce joy" that is reflected in her person, in her verse ("I am Lucille,
which stands for light"), and even in the titles of collections such as *Good
News About the Earth* (1972), *Good Woman* (1987), and *The Book of Light*
(1993). A passionate and tireless teacher as well as Poet Laureate of
Maryland from 1979 to 1982, Clifton is also the mother of six and author of
numerous books of children's literature.

POMEGRANATE BOX 6099 ROHNERT PARK CA 94927

© Jill Krementz

Poets

PHOTOGRAPHS BY JILL KREMENTZ

SEAMUS HEANEY, New York, N.Y., April 16, 1996
Seamus Heaney (b. 1939) came to poetry with the quiet dignity and
focused eye of the craftsmen and laborers who populate his verse. In
"Digging," which opens his first book, *Eleven Poems* (1965), he
compares his efforts in the writing trade to those of his father and
grandfather, diggers of Ireland's rich peat deposits. A reverence for the
soil and a love of pure language are uppermost in Heaney's work,
which includes *Wintering Out* (1973), *Field Work* (1979), *Seeing Things*
(1991), and *The Spirit Level* (1996). Heaney was awarded the Nobel
Prize in literature in 1995.

POMEGRANATE BOX 6099 ROHNERT PARK CA 94927

© Jill Krementz